The Poetry of A Preacher

Dr. Bobby Roger

Composed over a lifetime.

Put together in August of 2022

Preface

I have always loved poetry. Maybe it is because I also love music. There is something about the meter—the rhythm and beat of a poem that draws me in. Being a preacher, it may sound a little strange that one of my favorite poems of all time is Edgar Allen Poe's, *The Raven*. It was written in 1845, and I remember having to memorize the first stanza when I was in school. (Wow—that was a long time ago now!)

Once upon a midnight dreary, while I pondered, weak and weary,
Over many a quaint and curious volume of forgotten lore,
While I nodded, nearly napping, suddenly there came a tapping,
As of someone gently rapping, rapping at my chamber door.[1]

What a great opening verse! It has the elements I mentioned plus one more piece of a poem that makes poetry complete. It rhymes. Poetry without rhyming words never sits well with me. I think they call that prose. Here is an example of bad poetry.

Roses are red. Violets are bluc.
Sugar is sweet and so is birthday cake.

OUCH! I cringe at non-rhyming poetry the same way I do when fingernails go across a chalkboard. (Not everyone will remember that

[1] books.eserver.org/poetry/poe/raven.html/view?searchterm=raven

wonderful experience, but I do.) Poetry must rhyme—that is my opinion and I am sticking with it!

I also love limericks. They have a great meter, they rhyme, and they are also funny. That is a perfect combination. They are easy to write and can be written right on the spot. I was sitting in a college classroom years ago and wrote a quick one about one of the students that was giving me a hard time. It was all in good fun. Here it is.

There once was a fellow named Lynn
Whose life was loaded with sin.
He tried to be nice, which wouldn't suffice,
'Cause heaven still won't let him in!

I hope that made you at least chuckle.

Enough of that. I have written a good number of poems over the years; and so, I decided to put them into a book if for no other reason than to have them all together in one place for my family to read at some point in the future. Many of these poems have been written while I have been sitting in my office, working on a sermon. A few have been written in my mind while driving down the road.

One thing I know for sure is that the Lord gets credit for them. He has given me the ability to write each word along the way. You will see that I especially love to write Christmas poems. I try to write at least one new one each year. As you read through this collection, may your heart be blessed and drawn a little bit closer to Jesus Christ. To God be the glory!

Table of Contents

Christmas Poems

Christmas Peace

The Christmas season is here again
With hopes on earth of peace to men;
But as you look the world around,
There is no peace-it can't be found.

It can't be found when people say
We don't want Christ in Christmas day;
And they reject the herald Word—
The message that the shepherds heard.

It can't be found in those who think
That Christmas cheer comes in a drink
And so they chase their cares away
While missing Christ and His birthday.

It can't be found in shopping malls—
Just going up and down those halls
And running ragged day and night
You leave Christ out—that can't be right.

And even if there were a chance
You found the gift that made you dance
And thought that it was just the one—
Without the Lord, it'd be no fun.

(continued on next page)

You can't spell Christmas without Christ
No matter how it's diced or sliced;
And trying hard to find real peace
Without this Christ—your search won't cease.

For He alone can reach inside
And in your heart let peace abide;
And bring the peace you really need;
And free you from your sin indeed.

So put Christ in your Christmas plans
And put your life in Jesus' hands.
Just celebrate the Savior's birth
And you will find your peace on earth.

Keeping Christ in Christmas

What would Christmas be today if Christ were taken out?
If He were missing from the scene what would we sing about?
Joy to the World would lose its joy and *Silent Night* would be
Just that—a silent night—that's all—no joy, no mirth, no glee.

O Come Let Us Adore Him now would lose its certain flare
And certainly we could not find the song that's in the air.
The manger hymn that tells of where the infant Savior lay
Would not be sung, no, not at all, it would be far away.

And what about the drummer boy who beats his drum with hope?
There'd be no new-born king to see--in darkness men would grope.
For there would be no message on the mountains to proclaim;
No herald angels singing if we take away Christ's name.

Oh Little Town of Bethlehem would simply be a place
That very few would know about—there'd be no Savior's face.
And what would Mary need to know? Why say, "*What Child is This?*"
If Christ is not in Christmas, then why bother with this bliss?

But I, for one, refuse to bow to liberals and the press
Who want to tell me, "Take Christ out!" I won't! I must confess!
I'll celebrate My Lord and Christ—the carols I will sing
That speak His name—He's Jesus Christ, Immanuel, and King!

What Really Counts

Christmas day will soon be here
And, Oh in such a hurry.
It could be taken all in stride
But most of us just worry—
Going here and running there
And spending all our money.
Commercialism reigns as king
But doesn't that seem funny?

For it was not such worldly gain
That first brought Christmas cheer;
Nor was it jolly ol' Saint Nick
Or Rudolph, his red-nosed reindeer.
But it was angels telling of
A manger where there lay
A little babe—Immanuel—
It was the Lord's birthday.

Now that's the theme of Christmas time
My friends, that really counts;
And we must always think of that
As Christmas pressure mounts.
Remember God's sweet precious gift,
Salvation we hold dear,
And have a very, Merry Christmas
And a very blessed New Year!

It Was A Baby

What was it that the shepherds came to Bethlehem to see?
What was it made them leave their flocks and all so quickly flee?
What was it that the angels said that drew them to their word?
Oh yes, it was a baby: Jesus Christ the Lord!

What was it made the angels stir the shepherds in the night?
What was it caused a heavenly glow and lit the sky so bright?
What was it made the angels lift their praise in on accord?
Oh yes, it was a baby: Jesus Christ the Lord!

What was it made the wise men travel long and from afar?
What was it drew them to the east and chase a shining star?
What was it made them give the best that money could afford?
Oh yes, it was a baby: Jesus Christ the Lord!

What is it that we celebrate as Christians on the earth?
What is it making us so glad giving us such mirth?
What is it causing choirs world-wide to carol and to sing?
Oh yes, it is a baby: Jesus Christ the King!

Oh yes, it is a baby that does all this and more
But it's more than just a baby that we honor and adore.
We honor One Who gave His life according to God's Word.
He's more than just a baby: He's Jesus Christ the Lord!

The Wise Men

When the wise men took their journey
To behold the newborn King
In their heart there was a yearning
Just to worship him and sing.

To the King they brought their treasures
Of the finest, purest gold
For His worth they could not measure
And His reign would not grow old.

Now the frankincense was given
To the future priest that day
For to live a life in heaven
For their sins He'd have to pay.

Now the strangest gift they brought Him
Was the myrrh used for the dead.
Did they know the One before them
Would one day die in their stead?

And the truth is that this little king
They came to see that day
So impacted them and touched them
They went home another way!

It's More Than Just A Baby[2]

It's more than just a baby that brings us here today.
It's more than just the manger, the cradle, and the hay.
It's more than just the shepherds watching o'er their flock by night
When they heard the angels' voices and they saw the blinding light.

It's more than just a baby that brings us here today.
We're here to celebrate His birth—It is the Lord's birthday!
It's more than Jesus' birth we laud. We praise His life and more
That's why we're gathered here to sing, Oh Come Let Us Adore!

It's more than just a baby that brings us here today.
We're here to celebrate His death and resurrection day.
We're here to praise Him for the price He paid for all our sin
And to let Him know we're looking for the time He'll come again.

So, if you're here to only celebrate this baby's birth,
You've missed the point of why God sent this Savior to the earth.
We're here rejoicing in what God through Jesus did display
'Cause it's more than just a baby that brings us here today!

---

[2] This poem, though written in 90's, was set to music as a part of the 2021 Christmas cantata of Calvary Baptist Church. I also composed the score and narration.

I Am The Bread Of Life[3]

I am the Bread of Life
Sent down from God above
I am the living manna
Send down by God's great love
I am the bread of eternal life
O taste and you shall see

I am the Bread of Life
My flesh to you I give
I am the bread that you must eat
So you may truly live
I am the everlasting bread
O taste and you shall see

I am the Bread of Life
My body and my blood
I am the perfect sacrifice
My blood, the crimson flood
I am the way, the truth, the life
O taste and you shall see

[3] This was specifically written as a song for the 2021 Christmas cantata. It has also been sung in conjunction with communion.

A Christmas Poem

The Christmas season—it draws near—
a time that's filled with joy and mirth;
But some will find it hard to smile.
Someone they love is not on earth.

The joy of having them around
made celebrating all it's worth
But now they're gone—you've lost the joy
of singing of our Savior's birth.

Oh, don't forget the story
of the shepherds on a star-lit hill
Who were the first to hear about
God's peace an empty heart could fill;

For when Christ came the angels brought
a message filled with peace—good will.
For He alone could calm a storm
and say to it, "Storm, peace be still."

Christmas Carols to You

It's Christmas—yes, it's Christmas time
It's Christmas once again—
The time we celebrate God's peace
And goodwill to all men.
The time when Christ carols line the airwaves
And the malls:
Songs like *Rudolph*, *Jingle Bells*,
And a favorite, *Deck the Halls*.

Do You Hear What I Hear?
Christmas songs sung o'er the earth;
But the melodies I love the best
Tell of the Savior's birth.
Oh Come Let Us Adore Him!
Let the sounding joy repeat.
Go Tell It On The Mountain…
In the valleys…in the street!

Don't let this Christmas season pass
And catch you unaware
And *God Rest Ye Merry Gentlemen*
Becomes a desperate prayer!
Take *Silent Night*, *Joy To The World*,
And sing them with much cheer.
Have Yourself a Merry Little Christmas
And of course, a blessed New Year!

The Baby

She held the baby in her arms with gladness in her heart
For Mary knew just Who He was—She'd known it from the start.
An angel came and brought her news about this special birth.
The holy baby in her womb was God sent down to earth.

Now Joseph also got to hold the baby on that day.
"Don't be afraid to take this wife," He'd heard the angel say,
"For that which is conceived in her is of the Holy Ghost;"
And when he learned just who that was, I'm sure his heart did boast!

The shepherds saw the baby in the crib in swaddling clothes
And knew the vision they had seen was more than just some prose.
They'd clearly heard the angels' words and they just had to tell
That Christ the Lord was born that day—a story you know well.

And hopefully you see the same great truth these people saw
And still respond to Jesus' birth in holiness and awe
And share the special feeling that has given such great cheer
To all who know this Christmas truth and hold it oh so dear!

The Poem of Carols

It's Christmas time again, and as my tradition goes,
I write another Christmas poem (some might just call it prose).
I don't know how this started (the poems that I do write);
I sit right down with pen in hand and close my eyes real tight!

And then the words just come to me and so I write them down
And try to make a rhyming phrase so readers will not frown.
The verses may be three or four or maybe even five;
So, here I go again this year—my rhyming Christmas jive!

I love this special time of year—the joy that Christmas brings
The lights, the bells, the joyful songs that every caroler sings.
Joy to The World and *Silent Night—Good Christian Men, Rejoice;*
And *Angels We Have Heard On High.* I hear them lift their voice!

I Heard the Bells On Christmas Day; O Come, Emmanuel;
O Little Town of Bethlehem; and sure, *The First Noel;*
What Child Is This? The song does ask this question long ago;
We wonder as we sing the song named, *Mary, Did You Know?*

"*It Came Upon The Midnight Clear,*" that glorious song of old;
"*While Shepherds Watched Their Flocks By Night*" and kept them in their fold.
And then the song that celebrates *The Birthday of A King.*
How Great Our Joy—the songs don't stop—the *Herald Angels Sing*!

The COVID Christmas Poem[4]

T'was the day before Christmas and all through the house,
I wondered and pondered along with my spouse
About what would happen—we both mused the same;
Just what would occur if Santa Claus came.

Would he wear a mask—a shield oe'r his face;
Or not come at all—not come to our place?
Would he fear the virus or maybe the flu?
Now just what would this Christmas character do?

And if he did come—did come to our door—
Would he wash his hands and then walk on our floor?
Would each gift he brought be sanitized clean?
In this COVID world just imagine the scene!

And if we would wake while he's still by the tree,
And we all tried to greet him with joy and with glee;
Would he just shake his head and sternfully say?
"You know the rule—stay six feet away!"

(continued on next page)

[4] This was not written to offend anyone or make a statement. With 2020 being the first Christmas with COVID, I just wanted to have a little fun with some of the COVID "rules."

"Now go back to bed. Let me finish my work."
I'd say, "Mr. Claus, you have gone way berserk!
It's Christmas—that's something that's good and not bad
It's time to rejoice and be happy and glad."

Now I know that my story is fiction at best,
But how people act is really the test.
So, don't let this COVID stuff dampen your day
For Christmas is still about Jesus' birthday!

Go celebrate Christmas with many or few
And honor the Lord—that's just what we'll do.
We'll sing Christmas carols—the songs we all love,
And gratefully praise our great God above.

God's Sacrificial Lamb[5]

The prophecy came such a long time ago to a man who was named Abraham
That God would provide on a mountain one day Himself as a sacrificed lamb.
The years passed away and the lamb had not come—some two thousand years I would say—
And then on a night while shepherds stood watch they heard of a special birthday.

God's glory shined bright as the good news was shared—the Lamb had arrived on the earth!
"The Savior is born," they heard angels say. "Come see the place of His birth!"
And so, they arose and went in great haste to see where this promised Lamb lay;
And in a stone manger and swaddled in cloth, they found the Messiah that day.

The shepherds were thrilled as they told of His birth, but one thing was unclear to them:
Just how this young baby would grow up to be their promised and sacrificed Lamb.
A few years did pass and we read of a man whose message began to unfurl.
"Behold," he did say, "the [great] Lamb of God that takes away the sin of the world."

(continued on next page)

[5] This poem was written after preaching a sermon on The Sacrificial Lamb of Bethlehem during the 2021 Christmas season. I mentioned that someone ought to write a poem about this—so, I did.

And indeed, we would see the man we call Jesus, the Lamb that was sent from above,
Being nailed to a cross to die for our sins—a great sacrifice of His love.
And later we see, in John's Revelation, this blood and the Lamb that was slain;
But He is not dead—He's standing instead—we know He is living again!

But back to the promise made long, long ago to the man who was named Abraham—
The promise that God would provide on a mount Himself as a sacrificed lamb.
Remember the name of the One who would come for it tells us the name of this man.
Immanuel—God with us—It's God in the flesh! The Lamb is the great "I am."

No Christmas Bling

I walked around a retail store—observed its Christmas shelves—
And saw the message they did preach 'bout Santa and his elves.
Oh yes, they had the reindeer too, the sleigh and all its fluff;
With flashing lights and ornaments, all decked with shiny stuff.

The carols played so joyfully—the jingle bells did "jing"
And you could hear the many shoppers oh so quietly sing;
And as they shopped they'd "ooh" and "ah" o'er all the things they saw.
The Christmas bling seemed just the thing that mattered to them all.

But something else was there that day which had a different look
For I discovered something else stocked in a tiny nook.
It wasn't shining, bright, or lit—just lay there on the shelf
But the story that it pictured is a miracle in itself.

The manger scene I found proclaims a story of a birth
When God above invaded time and came to live on earth;
But more than that it pointed to a future time for men
When Jesus would grow up and die—to pay for all our sin.

I know that there are many folk who know this truth so well
But tend to put it on a shelf—forget God's love to tell!
Not meaning to, they get caught up in worldly Christmas bling,
And Jesus stays inside that nook while bells on bobtail ring.

So, let's be careful as we now approach this time of year
When we should long for peace on earth and spread the Christmas cheer
That comes from knowing more than just the baby in the hay.
We know that He is Christ the Lord! He's God in every way!

The Day After Christmas[6]

T'was the day after Christmas and all through the house
All the children were restless like dad and his spouse
For all the things promised to bring Christmas cheer
Were now one day old and no peace did appear.

"Buy this," said the ad, "buy this for your son
And he will have hours and hours of fun;
And this is the thing that you need for your girl
Many days of great joy will this doll house unfurl."

"Get this for your wife," oh how the ad pleaded;
And you were convinced that it's just what she needed
To make her so happy—to make life complete—
With all these great gifts life would ever be sweet!

Of course for yourself you found just the right gift
To boost all your spirits and give you a lift.
You just had to have it—other gifts would not do;
And then like the others, it no longer was new.

Tis the day after Christmas and instead of the thrills
Your life is no better but you still have the bills.
Does this scene sound familiar? Am I missing the mark?
Do you find all those presents too soon lose their spark?

(continued on next page)

[6] This poem, written in 1999, is one of my all-time favorites that I have written.

Perhaps it is time that we take a fresh look
At the story of Christmas that's found in God's Book
And realize that presents are not what we need
But only His presence will bring peace indeed.

For it was that message of peace and goodwill
That stirred shepherds' hearts as they watched from a hill
And rejoiced as the first Christmas story was told
Of a gift that would last and never grow old.

So may the day after Christmas be different this year
As you focus on Him Who said, "Be of good cheer!"
And while other gifts fade and their warmth may grow cold
Remember God's gift that never grows old!

The Wise Men

When the wise men took their journey
To behold the newborn King
In their heart there was a yearning
Just to worship him and sing.

To the King they brought their treasures
Of the finest, purest gold
For His worth they could not measure
And His reign would not grow old.

Now the frankincense was given
To the future priest that day
For to live a life in heaven
For their sins He'd have to pay.

Now the strangest gift they brought Him
Was the myrrh used for the dead.
Did they know the One before them
Would one day die in their stead?

And the truth is that this little king
They came to see that day
So impacted them and touched them
They went home another way!

New Year’s
Poems

New Year's Poem[7]

What lies ahead in the coming days
As we head for a brand new year?
With all the changes taking place
Some people live in fear.

Obamacare might be in place
And liberals will run wild;
I have to watch each thing I say
Or lawsuits could be filed.

I also hear that in the sky
Blood moons will soon appear.
Does all this mean we should expect
Our Lord to come next year?

I can't say, "Yes, I know for sure
That we'll be heaven bound;"
But I know the things that I must do
To faithfully be found:

Be steadfast in my Christian walk
To pray and read God's Word
And make each thing I say and do
Show Jesus is my Lord!

---

[7] I must admit that this poem may give a hint of my political persuasion and my eschatological position!

The Year Not Traveled

Another year will soon arrive. It is a gift from God
And we will face a brand new path that we have never trod.
It might bring us a life of joy that's filled with peace and gain,
Or we could struggle day by day and have some times of pain.
But does it really matter if we're walking with the Lord
And finding strength and comfort in the pages of His Word?
He said He'd never leave us or forsake us—that we know;
And that He'd be with us each day while on this earth we go.
So, rest in Him and let Him lead you day by day and more
For next year is a place that we have never been before!

A Poem for 2017

Two-0-seventeen—just what will it bring?
Now that New Year's is finally around.
Will I see my dream? Will I reach my goals?
These great resolutions abound

And I have my eyes on some wonderful things
that I very much want to achieve.
The thinking is clear that this world wants to teach:
success will be there—just believe.

Now some folk may say that this thinking is right—
believing is part of the game—
And setting a mark—a target ahead—
is exactly the right way to aim.

But one question I ask is for all to peruse—
it's one thing we all need to see.
Do these new aspirations I plan to pursue—
do these dreams come from God or from me?

Of course I do know, that though I believe,
it's Whom I believe in counts most;
And I cannot focus my faith on myself. In God—
that is where faith must boast.

(continued on next page)

For I know for sure that the plans I pursue
are nothing if it's not God's will,
If I forge ahead without God involved,
I'm pushing a rock up a hill.

And so as I come to another New Year
and consider what all lies ahead
I won't trust myself—I'll place all my faith
in Jesus who rose from the dead.

I'll stay in His Word and do all I can
to walk with the Lord through this land
And make His plans mine—not my will be done—
as He guides me along with His hand.

My 2020 New Year's Poem

Have a Happy, Happy New Year! O how oft we hear that phrase
As we enter in a brand new year—a year of unseen days.
Will happiness enrich my days? Will gleefulness abound?
Will each new day that lies ahead come with a joyful sound?

It's true that's what we all pursue—it's what we really seek;
But God knows what we really need. That's why our plans are weak.
We think one way and God says, "No! My will is best for you.
So, trust me now with each new day. I pledge to see you through."

And when the new days set their sun and life has run its course,
You'll learn how much you're glad you made the Lord your greatest source;
And sing—you will—a new song with a fresh unhindered glee,
A song of praise for God's great grace that now your eyes can see!

My 2021 New Year's Poem[8]

Can it be so? Dare I proclaim, "This year is almost done?"
I know that you and I would say, "It's not been loads of fun."
It started out so perfectly, and things were looking well;
And then that COVID thing showed up—a bat right out of hell.

Some rules were made to keep us safe (at least that's what they said).
It won't be long—two weeks or three; a fourth (let's look ahead);
For nothing's changed though months have passed—the rules (they stay the same):
"Don't leave your home." "Put on that mask" "Your safety is our aim!"

"And now there is a shot," they say, "to keep you COVID-free;
But still, you have to wear that mask to keep you safe, you see,
Because there are some people who'll refuse to get that shot;
And truthfully, we do not know if it will work or not."

So, as we face another year of unknown things to come
And pray that all will have good health (we know where that comes from),
I'd say that God still reigns on high and loves us through His Son
Though some may think He is asleep and "2020-won!"

---

[8] This one shows my cynical side about COVID, I admit. As I put this book together, we are in 2022; and quite honestly, not a whole lot has changed. These battles continue with no clear answers being provided.

Inspirational
Poems

Ignorance Is No Excuse

It will not do if you should say,
"I did not know the law.
I had not heard. No one had said."
That will not work at all.

Your ignorance is no excuse
no matter what you say,
Especially when you face the Lord
That final judgment day.

Now you may say, "I don't believe
the truth that's plain and clear;"
Or willfully ignore that truth
When spoken to your ear.

But truth is truth—God's Word will stand—
Your unbelief is sin.
You best repent while you have time—
He's coming back again!

The Scarlet Thread

The Scarlet Thread of Jesus may not sparkle like pure gold
But it's a story in God's Word that never will grow old.
It's not about religion or traditions made by man.
The Scarlet thread is Jesus—He is heaven's perfect Lamb!

It speaks about our Savior's blood—the cross of Calvary—
Revealing God's great mercy flowing from the rugged tree.
It sings of God's amazing grace—a sinless sacrifice.
God's love: It's just the trail of blood of His son, Jesus Christ.

The Scarlet Thread of which I speak—beginning to the end—
Tells the story of redemption—how God takes away our sin.
It's a flowing stream, a fountain, an eternal cleansing flood.
The Scarlet Thread of Jesus is the gospel in His blood

God's Ways

The Lord sees our heartache from high up above;
And though we may wonder, He showers His love.
He knows what He's doing—He has a great plan
E'en when deepest darkness may cover a man.

His ways are much higher—He sees so much more
Than just today's burdens that cut to the core
Or yesterday's problems we just can't forget;
The hurts we still feel—our grudges well kept.

He looks well beyond all these memories stained
With sorrows and troubles so deeply contained;
And says, "Please be patient. I'm still on the throne.
I'm working my will. You are not on your own."

So, hold fast your faith—do not doubt—just believe;
And one day you'll know what He had "up His sleeve.''
His ways are still perfect. You have much need to grow
And soon Who He is, you'll more perfectly know.

And when that day comes you will sing at your best
That you're thankful you stayed and finished the test.
You will see God's great hand and know in your heart
That where you are now, was His plan from the start!

Who is Jesus?

Was Jesus just a baby lying in a manger bed—
Just a young boy at a temple wowing priests with what He read?
Was Jesus just a simple man who walked upon this earth,
Doing good to all who met Him--bringing joy and peace and mirth?
Was Jesus plainly just a man who thought He was divine?
Was He only just a prophet whom with God He did align?
Did He really heal the sick—cause the blinded man to see;
Open deaf ears, raise the dead, was He Who He claimed to be?
And when He hanged upon the cross, did He die a mortal man?
Did He really rise up from the dead according to His plan?

You see, the way that you respond to all these questions here
Will determine where you go one day—the answer must be clear.
You cannot fudge on Who He is or what He came to do.
You must believe that He is God—the One that died for you;
And that He rose up from the grave—oh that's important too!
He is the One sent down from God, our Father up above,
He came to give His life for us—to show unfailing love!
Now you must get the answer right while on this earth you trod.
Who is this man? He's Jesus Christ, the son of the living God!

The Day After Thanksgiving!

Tis' the day after Thanksgiving and all through the house
The family is dragging, (maybe even a mouse);
For all the food eaten has lulled them to be
Lethargic and sluggish—a poor sight to see.

The turkey was juicy—and cooked oh so right.
The dressing—it could have been eaten all night!
The taters were great (both mashed and the yams)
And what can I say 'bout the gravy and hams!

The desserts--my oh my--let me say it again.
The desserts—well, now that's where I started to sin
'Cause I just couldn't stop—pumpkin pie and pecan
Topped with Cool Whip so rich I could go on and on…

But we are all stuffed like the turkey we ate.
Black Friday is here and I think I'll just wait.
There's no use getting up and fighting the crowd
After eating so much—that move's not allowed

(continued on next page)

So, I say, “Let’s stay home.” (I’ve looked in the fridge).
There are leftovers there—and a lot, not a smidge!
And I feel a call for the family to meet
‘Round the table again—one more Thanksgiving treat!

We’re so blessed with the bounty from God up above.
He has given so much as an act of His love;
But the greatest thing ever our Father has done
Is to send Jesus Christ. He sent us His Son!

He died on the cross and shed all His blood
So we could be saved through that red, crimson flood;
And while we have basked in a Thanksgiving feed,
We say, “Thank you, Lord. You’ve met our soul’s need!”

Poems
Set to Music

I have written over 100 songs—mostly Christian and/or Gospel songs. The lyrics of my songs are basically poems that have been transformed into a melody. I want to share a few of them with you, hoping they will both bless and encourage you. At times, the precise meter of a traditional poem may be a little off in these lyrics. If that is the case, it is because of the melody line or the switch to a little bit different melody line for the chorus; but when it is sung, it all comes together and makes sense.

Before I get to the serious poems set to music, I have to include one of my favorite non-spiritual poems. It was written back in the 1980's when Kim and I lived in a trailer house that had an all too familiar problem with cock roaches. We tried over-the-counter methods of dealing with them without success. Then we met a fellow servant of the Lord who just happened to be in the extermination business. His name is Bobby Meek. He came to our home and totally eliminated the cock roach problem. In honor of him and his business, I wrote this song and told him he could use it for the theme song for his business. (I do not think he actually even did that but we did have a good laugh at the thought of it.) Here it is in all its glory!

No more roaches; oh, it makes me kind of sad
Just to think that there's no roaches in our cozy little pad.
No more ugly bugs to step on when we enter in the door—
No more ugly splotches on the kitchen floor.

No more roaches; oh, just think how it could be
When you open up your cabinets and not a roach you see.
No more roaches on the countertop no matter where you seek—
And we owe it all to Mister Bobby Meek!

Part of the Family

Just like a ship that's tossed by the wind,
My life was a drifting, lost in my sin;
But then Master set my life free.
He made me a part of His family.

One day, in heaven, we'll gather up there,
And praise Him, and thank Him; God's glory we'll share.
Simply because He made us to be
A joint heir with Jesus in His family.

Calvary

I had wandered in sin's darkness; I had suffered pain and woe
Even though I'd heard the story of how Jesus loved me so.
But I still did not know him till one night upon my knees,
I met this man called Jesus at the cross of Calvary,

I don't have the words to tell you just what Jesus means to me
Ever since He took my burdens; ever since He set me free.
It's been a life of hope and joy, and love beyond degree
All because I met the Master at the cross of Calvary.

All Things Work Together

Well my trials were so heavy and my burdens weighed me down.
I thought that I had stood all that I could.
Then the Lord said, “Be patient weary pilgrim,
For all things work together for good.

Then the Lord turned my sorrows into gladness and to joy.
Now I’m praising God the way I know I should.
For when Jesus turns your mourning into laughter,
You know all things work together for good.

Now I’m on my way to heaven and I’m singing as I go,
“Hallelujah, Praise the Lord, for God is good;”
And I know that when I see my blessed Savior
Why He works this way will all be understood.

Aren't You Getting Homesick?

When John the Revelator saw the scenes of glory
What a glorious sight he did behold
He saw the holy city coming down out of heaven
And he saw a street made of pure gold.

He saw a place of splendor like a royal bride's beauty
A city that was made by God's own hand
Where there would be no sickness, no sorrow, sin, or sadness
No crying, pain, or death in this perfect land.

He heard God's invitation to the ones who would be thirsting
To take the water of life for it is free!
He heard the voice of Jesus, saying, "Surely, I come quickly."
And John said, "Come right now!" excitedly.

Chorus

Aren't you getting homesick for your home in glory?
Aren't you getting tired of living here below?
Aren't you getting homesick for that place called heaven?
Even so Lord, come now, I want to go.

His Grace is Sufficient

Once a man named Paul had a thorn in his flesh
In sorrow his heart did abide
To the Lord did he pray, "Will you take it away?"
To his question the Lord replied.

So Paul he'd glory in his infirmities
That Jesus might be glorified.
Though his valleys were deep, a joy he did keep
For he lived with these words deep inside.

Now when you go through a storm and your valleys are low
And your mountains, well, they just seem too tall.
You are weary and worn, defeated and torn;
Just remember what the Lord told Paul.

Chorus

"My grace is sufficient for thee.
My strength is made perfect in weakness."
So when you go through a storm,
Keep your eyes on the Lord.
His grace is sufficient for thee.

I Am Redeemed[9]

I was a sinner dead in my sin
Lost in the darkness, blinded within
Then Jesus shined His grace down on me
I was redeemed. Praise God I can see!

I was so guilty. I was undone.
God's Spirit drew me to His precious Son
With great love He loved me—He died on the cross
Now I'm redeemed, and I'm no longer lost!

The Lord's up in heaven. The Lamb on His throne.
The One slain for sinners Who made me His own.
One day I'll see Him there face to face.
Redeemed forever—still saved by His grace!

chorus

Oh hallelujah   I am redeemed
My sins forgiven. My soul's been set free.
Praise to the Lord, the great I am.
I am redeemed by the blood of the Lamb!

[9] This song has become a favorite to sing at Calvary Baptist.

I Am Saved!

I am redeemed by the blood of the Lamb—
all my sins washed away I am saved.
I was in bondage—my sin had me bound
by God's grace I'm no longer enslaved.
My sins are forgiven I'm headed for heaven
because of the love that He gave.
Jesus is Lord—I proclaim by His Word,
I am saved, saved, saved!

Jesus came down from His heavenly home
and he walked on this earth among men,
Knowing one day He would die on a cross
so that I could be saved from my sin.
Loving me freely He gave up His life
so that I could have peace deep within.
Oh what a Savior—He gave me His favor—
I'm saved, saved, saved!

One day He's coming from glory to take me
to my home that's up in the sky
Jesus will come in the clouds to receive me—
away up to heaven I'll fly
I know I will be in that heavenly place
and forever my Lord glorify.
I called on His name. I'm no longer the same. I am saved, saved, saved!

Come Magnify the Lord[10]

I will bless the Lord at every time;
Songs of praise shall always be in me.
My soul shall boast about the Lord sublime.
Lord, with a humble heart I'm glad in Thee.

When troubles all around me now may fall
I go to Him who saves me from my fears;
And on the precious name of God I call.
And He, in love, just wipes away my tears.

Oh, taste and see the Lord, that He is good.
Lord, blessed is the man that trusts in Thee.
For when I walk with You the way I should
Then there will be no want that comes to me.

Chorus

Oh, come and magnify the Lord with me.
Let us now exalt His name together.
Let us magnify Him as our King.
Lord, we want to lift You up forever!

---

[10] This poem/song is based on Psalm 34.

I Know That I'm Saved

I heard of a Savior
Who'd give me His favor
If I would just call on His name.
So, I knelt at His cross
Because I was so lost
And now I am no longer the same.

Though Jesus did save me
The fact He forgave me
Is awesome oh how can it be.
His love's overwhelming,
His grace so compelling,
He saved me praise God I am free.

And one day in glory
We'll all share His story
And bask in the light of His love;
Rejoicing together,
And praising forever
Our great God in heaven above.

The Son of God

He came to this world; on this earth, He stood
And He lived and He died as no other man could
For He lived in perfection as all of us should.
He was the Son of God.
When He came He knew He would be crucified
For men walked in darkness, His love they denied.
So alone He suffered, and bled, and died.
He was the Son of God.

When John saw this Man he said, “Behold the Lamb
That takes away sins; Oh, what a sinner I am.
And I’m not worthy at all to baptize this Man
He is the Son of God.”
At the foot of the cross a soldier stood by,
And he looked on our Lord and watched Him die;
Then he saw a great truth and in awe he cried,
“This man was truly the Son of God!”

Let Me Go

Lord, I see the Brazen Altar where the sacrifice was made
And it tells me of the precious blood where the price for sin was paid.
There's the Laver of Your holy Word that cleanses me within.
In the Outer Court I cannot stay, I want to enter in.

Though surrounded by Your righteousness, by that fence so pure and white,
I know there's so much more to see—I want to see that light
That shines on the Table and the Altar by the Veil.
By the blood of Christ I'll enter in and there I shall prevail.

Let me go into that Holy Place
Where I can meet God face to face
And see the blood on the Mercy Seat
From the cross of Calvary.
Let me bask in the holiness
Of the One Who is so glorious;
And let His shining presence fall on me,
As I come before the Lord most Holy.

The Real Question

It's not a question of how rich you are or the things that you have achieved.

It's not a question of who you may be or the honors you have received.

It's not a question of what you have done or who you hope to be.

But it's a question of do you know Christ? Are you sure you'll live eternally?

It's not a question of going to church saying, "Hallelujah" or an "Amen."

It's not a question of doing good works or living a life free of sin.

It's not a question of how loud you sing the songs that praise the Lord up above.

But it's a question of do you know Christ? Have you trusted in the gift of God's love?

It's not a question of how smart you are or the sermons you may have heard.

It's not a question of how much you know about the Bible, God's Holy Word.

It's not a question of how much you tithe, how long our fast, or how much you pray.

But it's a question of do you know Christ? Does He really live in your heart today?

(continued on next page)

Chorus

What have you done with the gift of God's love?
Do you really trust in Jesus' name?
Or do you just speak the language of heaven?
Salvation to you is a game.
Answer this question today if you will,
"Have you really done what Jesus said?"
Confess with thy mouth the Lord,
Believe in thine heart that Jesus Christ has been raised from the dead.

I Can Do All Things Thru Christ

Defeated, I was defeated when I listened to the devil speak.
He told me that I was a loser, He told me that my faith was weak
And I believed him, and I couldn't become what the Lord wanted me to be
Until I read in God's Word that I could do all things thru Christ Jesus that strengthens me.

Tormented, I was tormented by my doubt and my homemade fears
For I believed, that I was a failure, my life was filled with tears
But praise the Lord, I was set free from bondage and I won the victory.
When I believed what I read that I could do all things thru Christ Jesus that strengthens me.

Chorus
I can do all things thru Christ Jesus that strengthens me.
For I know I belong to Him, with Him I'm a majority
In Jesus' name, I have been given all power and authority
I could do all things thru Christ Jesus that strengthens me.

Tag
Greater is He that is in me than he that is in the world
With the shield of faith, I have learned to quench the fiery darts that Satan's hurled
I've been made more than a conqueror. In the Lord, I now abide
I'm a child of God. How can I lose when I'm on the winning side?

It Won't Be Long

I can tell by your face you're getting tired of living here.
You're tired of all the heartache, the pain, and the tears;
And your burdens are heavy; well friend, just hang on
For it won't be long 'till He takes His children home.

Your sorrows are many and dark is your night;
And it seems there's no singing, it seems there's no light.
Well just look unto Jesus and He'll keep you strong,
And, it won't be long 'till He takes His children home.

Chorus
I can feel it in the air. I see the signs everywhere.
It's getting closer each day; soon, He's gonna take us away.
So, look up, head up high; your redemption draweth nigh
Oh, it won't be long 'till He takes His children home.

Lord I Need Your Mercy[11]

Lord, I need Your mercy
And Lord, I need Your grace
I need Your loving presence
To fill and bless this place
So far away I've wandered
And have failed to seek Your face
So, Lord, I need Your mercy
And Lord, I need Your grace

Chorus

Hear my prayer…I call upon Your name
Change me, Lord…I cannot stay the same
Cleanse my heart…please forgive me for my sin
Touch me, Lord, revive my heart again

[11] This is short chorus that we sing unto the Lord from time to time at Calvary Baptist.

Window of Grace

The Lord is rich in mercy to those who fear His name
His favor and His faithfulness forever stays the same
But often we do stumble and we fail to run the race
We need His hand of mercy—a window of His grace

The Lord just keeps on blessing—more than I could ever know
Not given me what I deserve as I walk this earth below
When I fail Him, He still loves me; all my sins He will erase
For He offers me His mercy—this window of His grace

Chorus
A moment of mercy—a window of grace
A time of repentance—to seek the Lord's face
As long as it's open—we must strive to embrace
This moment of mercy—this window of grace

You Are God[12]

When I think about Your name…the greatness it implies-
It tells me that You're holy…You're the only One that's wise
And I love to sing Your praises…And magnify Your name
To worship You forever…O Lord, that is my aim.

You're Jehovah, my provider…My shepherd and my guide
You are the Christ of Calvary…Where You gave Your life, and died
You're the resurrected Savior…Forgiver of my sin
You are the Lord of glory…And You're coming back again!

Chorus
You are God, You are King of kings
The Lord of lords, You are
You are Jesus…the great I Am
The bright and morning star
You're the everlasting Father
You're evermore the same
You are God.
How I love to praise Your name.

Tag
For Your name is higher than any other name I know
And Your love is greater
That's why I love you so
I will sing Your praises and lift your name on high
Oh, I love You, Jesus
It's You I glorify

[12] This is also one of the favorite songs we sing at Calvary Baptist.

The Rich Man in Hell[13]

Can you feel the flame? Can you feel the fire?
Burning in my soul – Burning every hour.
Can you feel the pain? Can you here the cries?
Everlasting fame – Ever in my eyes.

I am so afraid – I am so alone
But I have no friend – I am own my own.
I don't want to live – But I cannot die.
I cannot escape – Someone hear my cry.

I said no to God – And the blood He shed
I rejected Christ – Eternally I'm dead
Will you tell my friends – Oh, hey need to hear
Tell my family too. Please don't let them come here.

Chorus

If I could have just a drop of cool water
For I am tormented in this flame
Please someone give me some relief from my torture
For everyday this fire is the same.

Will you tell my friends
They don't have to go
To this awful place
God loves them so

---

[13] I wrote this poem in the 80's during a sermon on the subject of hell. The preacher remarked that no one ever sings a song about hell; so, while he was preaching, the Lord gave me the tune and lyrics for this song/hymn. Since he was preaching on hell that night, I went to the piano and sang it for the first time during the invitation. It is obvious that it comes from Luke 16:19-31.

I Want to Be Like Him

I want to be like Him in the way I talk.
I want to be like Him in the way I walk.
I want to be like Him; I want to be like Him.
I want to be like Him in the way I sing.
I want to be like Him in everything.
I want to be like Him; I want to be like Him.
I want to be like Him each and every day.
I want to be like Him in every way.
I want to be like Him; I want to be like Him.
I want to be like Him for I know I should.
I want to be like Him, oh, I wish I could.
I want to be like Him; I want to be like Him.

Chorus

For He has saved me and He gave me eternal life;
Forgave me, set me free from my sinful life;
Redeemed me by His blood, by the blood of the Lamb.
Yes, He has saved me, now I walk in abundant life;
Forgave me, born again, it's a brand-new life;
Redeemed me by His blood, by the blood of the Lamb.

Appendix A: Salvation

This book would not be complete without giving you, the reader, and invitation to begin a living relationship with Jesus Christ. I invite you to read the next few pages prayerfully and carefully.

Jesus spoke these words in Luke 13:3: “Except ye repent, ye shall all likewise perish.” That is a serious statement. Repentance is the key to salvation; and so, I want to take a few moments to share with you God’s simple plan of salvation.

It starts with recognizing that we are sinners. That should be easy because we all stand on equal ground at this point. The Scriptures point out that “all have sinned, and come short of the glory of God.”[14] God’s commandments have been broken. We are guilty; and because of this, we are under the condemnation of death—we are destined to perish.

“The wages of sin is death; but the gift of God is eternal life through Jesus Christ our Lord.”[15] Praise God that He has provided a gift for us—one that cancels the debt we owe and gives us eternal life! This is God’s free gift. That is indeed good news; which is the definition of the word, “gospel.” In writing about this gospel, the Apostle Paul tells us “that Christ died for our sins according to the scriptures.”[16] That means that when Jesus died on the cross, He was dying in our place—paying the wages of our sins; but we must remember that this is a gift.

---

[14] Romans 3:23.

[15] Romans 6:23.

[16] I Corinthians 15:3.

In order for a gift to do me any good, I have to receive it and open it up. If I leave it on the table, I gain no benefit from it. That is the same thing with this wonderful gift from God. John 3:16 expounds on this. "For God so loved the world, that he gave his only begotten Son, that whosoever believeth in him should not perish, but have everlasting life." The gift of God was His son, Jesus, dying on the cross of Calvary and it was given to us in love[17]; but again, we have to take this gift and make it our own.

Why do I need this gift? That is simple. If I reject this gift of love from God, I will perish. That means I will die as an unforgiven sinner and will spend eternity in hell. If I refuse to turn from my sin and turn to Jesus (this is repentance), I condemn myself to that kind of eternity.

On one occasion, Paul was speaking to a group of elders. He brought a simple message to them. It was easy to understand: "repentance toward God, and faith toward our Lord Jesus Christ."[18] That sums up the gospel message. You must turn to God and place your faith in the Lord Jesus Christ. After all, He is the One that died for you and is the only One that can save you.

Paul gave us a definitive word on salvation in Romans 10:9-10. "That if thou shalt confess with thy mouth the Lord Jesus, and shalt believe in thine heart that God hath raised him from the dead, thou shalt be saved. For with the heart man believeth unto righteousness; and with the mouth confession is made unto salvation." (There is that word "heart" again!)

---

[17] Romans 5:8 tells us that God demonstrated His great love to us "while we were yet sinners."

[18] Acts 20:21.

You, of course, would not believe that Jesus rose from the dead unless you first believed that He died on the cross. Paul makes one more statement that gives us a final piece of the puzzle. He writes in Romans 10:13 these important words. "For whosoever shall call upon the name of the Lord shall be saved."

So, there you have it. Jesus loved you so much that He died on the cross to pay the price of death for your sins. Just as the Passover lamb's blood was put on the door posts of the Israelites' homes and protected them from the judgment of death the night God's judgment fell on Egypt, the blood of Jesus, God's perfect Lamb, was shed at Calvary to save anyone who would turn to Him from the eternal death he deserves because he is a sinner. That indeed is good news.

How about it? Have you ever repented—turned from your sins and placed your faith in the Lord Jesus Christ? If not, I want to give you the opportunity right now, as you are reading this, to do so. Admit to God you are a sinner and have broken His commandments. Tell Him you are sorry for your sins and you know you deserve to die and go to hell. Let Him know you believe He died on the cross for you and He rose from the dead. Confess you are willing to turn from your sins and your way of life and you want to turn to Him, making Him the Lord of your life. Thank Him for His gift of eternal life. Thank Him for hearing your prayer and saving you!

My friend, it really is that simple; but you must be willing to repent and turn to the Lord in faith. Do not wait for a better day. Do it now while you have the chance. The Holy Scriptures tell us in Second Corinthians 6:2: "Behold, now is the accepted time; behold, now is the day of salvation."

About The Author

Dr. Robert (Bobby) Roger was born in Big Spring, Texas and is a graduate of Big Spring High School. He attended Howard County Junior College there for three semesters and spent one semester at Hardin Simmons University in Abilene, Texas. During those first years of college, he answered God's call to the ministry and finished his early years of education at Criswell Bible College in Dallas. In May of 1979, Bobby graduated from Criswell with a BA degree in Biblical studies.

While going to Criswell, Bobby was asked to lead the music at FBC of Sunnyvale. It is there that he met a beautiful young lady who would one day be his wife. Kim and Bobby got married on May 12, 1979, the day before his college graduation. Two weeks later, they were serving in Slaton, Texas. Bobby served as the music and youth director of Westview Baptist Church. Jim Wilkerson, who had been Bobby's pastor as a teenager in Big Spring, was the pastor there. (He is a "retired" preacher now and is an active member of Bobby's church today!)

In June of 1981, Bobby and Kim moved to Sulphur Springs, Texas, where Bobby served as pastor of Trinity Baptist Church for seven years. While in Sulphur Springs, the Lord blessed them with their first three children: Amy, Nathan, and Stacy.

In June of 1988 and with Kim being eight months pregnant with their fourth and final child (Julie), the family moved to the very top of the Panhandle of Texas—Perryton, Texas, to be exact. Bobby served as the pastor of Southside Baptist Church there for over eleven years.

In July of 2000, God called Bobby to his present pastorate—Calvary Baptist Church in San Angelo, Texas. (At the writing of this book, he has served there over twenty-two years.) It is during this time that he went back to college. He would be a part of the online studies of Liberty University out of Lynchburg, Virginia. Taking several years to complete his education, Bobby receive an MDiv degree as well as an MAR degree. He followed that up with a DMin degree which he received in May of 2017. The area of specific studies at Liberty University was in Expository Preaching and Evangelism.

Kim and Bobby's children are all grown now and they are the proud grandparents of seven grandchildren. He has authored four other books. His first book, *The Lost Art of Revivals*, is the book form of his dissertation work at Liberty University. His other three books are also available on Amazon. They are *How to Harden Your Heart; The Rise, Fall, and Rise of The Apostle Peter;* and *The Four Second Comings of Jesus.*

You can contact him through his email: calvarypreacher@hotmail.com.

www.ingramcontent.com/pod-product-compliance
Lightning Source LLC
LaVergne TN
LVHW052055160826
845678LV00015B/3245

9798846884441